Out of the
Ocean

DEBRA FRASIER

Out of the Ocean

Voyager Books • Harcourt, Inc.

SAN DIEGO   NEW YORK   LONDON

With special thanks to Millie and George, who raised us all in the house by the ocean,
and to my editor and friend, Allyn Johnston, who grew up beside that other great ocean,
and to my neighbors, Margy and Jerry, who grew up on the Great Plains,
where the land stretches around us, like an ocean.

www.harcourt.com

First Voyager Books edition 2002
Voyager Books is a trademark of Harcourt, Inc., registered in the United States of America and/or other jurisdictions.

The Library of Congress has cataloged the hardcover edition as follows:
Frasier, Debra.
Out of the ocean/Debra Frasier [author and illustrator].
p.   cm.
Summary: A young girl and her mother walk along the beach and marvel at the treasures cast up by the sea and the wonders of the world around them.
[1. Beaches—Fiction.   2. Nature—Fiction.]   I. Title.
PZ7.F86540u   1998
[Fic]—dc20   96-5274
ISBN 0-15-258849-3
ISBN 0-15-216354-9 pb

H G F E D C

Printed in Singapore

The text type and display type were set in Gill Sans.
Color separations by Bright Arts, Ltd., Singapore.
Printed and bound by Tien Wah Press, Singapore
Production supervision by Sandra Grebenar and Wendi Taylor
Designed by Michael Farmer

For what my brother, Dan,
and the sea turtles want—

this sky

this sand

this ocean.

MY MOTHER SAYS you can ask
the ocean to bring you something.

If you look, she says,
you might find it.

Like the sun, she says.
She asks for it every morning
and there it is, rising up
out of the ocean.

Is it true? I ask her.
You can ask for anything?

Keep watching, she answers,
and the next day the sun rises up
out of the water one more time,
just like she wanted.

Can you ask the ocean
for something special?
I ask my mother.
Every day I ask for water,
she says, and look—
water everywhere.

Look how far the water stretches,
how it sails above us in
clouds bigger than cities.

And out there
we can see water falling
into the ocean all over again.

I know you can ask
the ocean for shells,
because every time we go
to the beach looking,
there they are,
tumbling end over end,
arriving empty,
most times worn
by the sand and waves.

But can you ask
the ocean for treasure?
I asked my mother.

Certainly, she said,
just be looking for it.

So when we found it,
we called it treasure—
that broken glass that has
rolled around on the ocean floor
until it's smooth and glowing.

Green and brown are easy to find,
but blue, that's special, and red,
the rarest of all, can make you
run all the way home just to
show someone you found it.

One day a splintered board painted
with a white stripe washed in—
just what we wanted for
the castle we were building.
That board found us
before we could even ask.

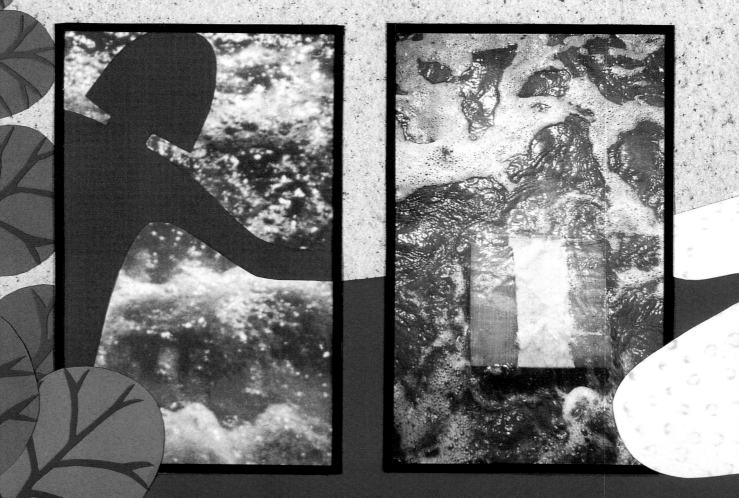

At the ocean things can
surprise you like that.

Walking this beach,
I've found pelican feathers,
a wooden shoe, floating glass balls,
skate egg pouches, plastic boats,

abandoned rafts,
two unbroken sea urchin shells,
messages curled inside bottles,
carved wooden floats...

... coconuts, sea turtle skulls,
a beam from a sunken ship, shark's teeth,
and a giant pile of tangled rope.

I've carried home all these things, and
each one turned out to be
just what I wanted.

But my mother,
she keeps asking
for things that
are too big to
carry home.

Sun. Water.
Silver moonlight.
The sound of waves.
Sea turtle tracks
at dawn.

Those things are
always here, I tell her.
You just have to
look for them.

She laughs and says
that now I know her secret.
It's not the asking.
It's the remembering to look.

And sometimes, she says,
the bigger the thing,
the easier it is to forget to see it.

I don't think I'll
ever forget to see
something as big as the sun.
Or the water.

But just to be sure, every day,
we help each other look.

An Ocean Journal

For over thirty-five years my family has lived just north of Vero Beach, Florida, in a house overlooking the warm waters of the great Atlantic Ocean. In that time four generations of us have walked the shoreline, finding things. Some of these things have delighted us, like delicate sea urchin shells or glass balls, and others have angered us, like thick patches of tar or a mangled sea turtle. Living here, we've learned that much of what goes into the ocean eventually washes out of the ocean somewhere else. Every high tide leaves a new array of objects on the beach, and each is like a chapter in a story. Our discoveries—some wonderful, others alarming—tell us much about our world and how we humans are affecting the land and water.

DEBRA FRASIER

If You Look, You Might Find It

Shells • A shell is the hard covering that was once excreted by a soft marine animal that needed protection underwater to survive. Two kinds of shells are most often found at this particular Florida beach: single spiral shells, called univalves, and clamlike shells, called bivalves. Only the sturdiest shells reach this shore without breaking to pieces because along the way they must cross sunken reefs, travel up a steep bottom incline, and tumble through constant wave action. Moon snail and conch shells are common, but the sand is most frequently dotted with the ponderous ark, shown in this picture. By the time a ponderous ark has tumbled to shore from its reef habitat, it has, like most bivalves, been split into two halves, and is bleached to a bright white.

Note in a Bottle • We have found several bottles containing notes, some thrown into the sea by individuals, and some from scientific studies. This one comes from an ocean current research project based in Miami. The Gulf Stream, one of the strongest ocean currents known, moves north off the coast of Florida. It is like a river inside the ocean, carrying warm waters from the Caribbean Sea. Around Cape Hatteras the current begins to move offshore, turning toward Portugal and Spain. This current was discovered by early sailors and served as a major path for explorers and traders returning to Europe. One bottle we found had traveled the Gulf Stream from the mouth of the Amazon River, where it had been thrown off a ship.

Wooden Shoe • As long as boats have sailed the sea, seamen have been losing things to the water. This shoe was hand-carved in the Netherlands tradition and probably fell off a fishing vessel from a Dutch port. It could have traveled the Gulf Stream from anywhere in the Caribbean or South American fishing fields.

Black Skate Egg Pouch • Sometimes called mermaid's or devil's purses, these buoyant egg cases are quite sturdy. Each pouch will hold one clearnose skate embryo while it develops. After nine weeks, if not washed to shore, the pouch will finally split open. A tiny skate will then unfold its triangular body and whiplike tail, slip out, and leave the pouch behind.

Glass Fishing Floats • Floats like these once supported the longlines and gill nets used in deep sea commercial fishing. Attached with braided rope coverings, the glass balls held up miles of fishing nets. A glass float's country of origin can be determined from its stamp, stopper, and seam. We have found glass floats lost from fishing ships traveling from European, Scandinavian, German, Japanese, and American ports. Most glass floats have been replaced by various plastics and Styrofoam, and now they are a very rare find on the Atlantic coast.

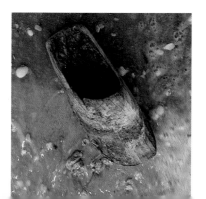

Sea Turtle Tracks • Although our family has lived by the sea for decades, sighting the tracks of tiny sea turtle hatchlings or evidence of a giant female's nesting crawl remains one of the most exciting finds at the beach. Loggerhead sea turtles hatch from nests dug high along sandy beaches. When the hatchlings scurry to the sea, they are no larger than a child's palm. They then "disappear" for the first years of life (researchers have not yet confirmed exactly where they feed during this time), "returning" as adolescent turtles, feeding along reef ledges. Loggerhead sea turtles eat jellyfish, crustaceans, and mollusks, and usually grow to weights of up to 350 pounds. After reaching maturity (somewhere between 18 and 30 years), a loggerhead swims, in early summer, back toward the beach where it hatched. The turtles mate offshore, and the female swims into the beach under the cover of darkness to dig a nest in the sand. She will lay between 80 and 150 eggs above the high-water mark, then return to the sea. The heavy turtle's nighttime crawl leaves a double set of deep tracks in the sand that lead to and from the buried nest.

A female loggerhead may nest five or six times during the nesting season. After six to eight weeks of warming in the hot sand, the eggs will hatch, and the tiny turtles will crawl to the sea, continuing the loggerheads' life cycle, as their ancestors have for some 150 million years.

From the moment they are deposited in the sand, turtle eggs are preyed upon by humans, foxes, and raccoons. The hatchlings can be attacked by gulls, crabs, and larger fish of all kinds. Once in the deep ocean the tiny turtles must make their own way without the help of their parents. It is estimated that for every 5,000 eggs laid, only one turtle will survive to grow to maturity.

The Atlantic beaches of central Florida are the nesting sites of the world's second-largest population of loggerhead turtles. One-quarter of all loggerhead nests in the United States are located here, from around Vero Beach to Melbourne Beach, 40 miles to the north. In 1994 nearly 30,000 nests were counted in this narrow band of coastline. Recently, in an unprecedented joint government-and-foundation effort, close to 500 acres along 9 miles of oceanfront land were purchased for the Archie Carr National Wildlife Refuge as a nesting sanctuary for sea turtles.

Driftwood • Wood that washes ashore is called driftwood and includes both natural wood and milled lumber. Salt water, sand, waves, and sun all work to alter and smooth the wood over time into beautiful shades of gray. We have found small, oddly shaped bits of wood, boxes with different languages painted on them, wooden steps, and even entire trees uprooted by storms.

Loggerhead Turtle Skull • Five of the world's eight species of sea turtles inhabit the coastal waters of the United States, but the loggerhead turtle is the most plentiful in this part of Florida. Nevertheless, their numbers are dwindling worldwide, and loggerheads are now listed as a threatened species in the United States. The primary threat to all sea turtles continues to be human activity. Fishing practices, the degradation of habitat by pollution, and overdevelopment of nesting areas all imperil these animals. Female sea turtles must lay their eggs in dry sand. Once the turtles are out of the ocean, their usually protective huge size leaves them defenseless because they move very slowly on land. This vulnerability has made them easy prey, especially for humans, who, over the last 200 years, have hunted turtles to the brink of extinction.

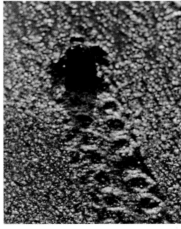

Carved Floats • This is one of several fishing net floats to arrive via the Gulf Stream from Caribbean boats. Each float is unique and carved of a light wood with a knob on top for attaching the net.

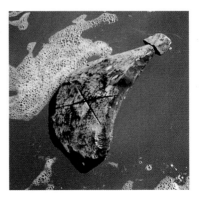

Burnished Glass • All kinds of glass bottles find their way to the ocean. Once the glass is broken, the pieces rub and tumble through the sand on their way to the shore. This burnishing gives the glass its jewel-like glow. Some people consider surf-worn glass to be a real treasure, collecting certain colors or sizes. One beach walker we know looks only for pieces that will fit through the neck of the tiny clear bottle he uses for storing his collection.

Sunken Ship • In 1715 eleven galleons of the Spanish Combined Armada sank on the offshore reefs here during a fierce hurricane. Their holds were filled with gold ingots, Chinese porcelain, and silver pieces of eight, all destined for the king of Spain. For 250 years the ships lay submerged in 15 to 30 feet of water just north of this beach. In the early 1960s searchers found and began to excavate the ships and their treasure. This massive beam arrived onshore after a storm. The iron ties marked it as part of a ship's construction, and testing proved it to be wood of Spanish origin, probably from around the early 1700s.

Pelican Feather • Although the brown pelican is an endangered species, it is plentiful in this part of Florida. Pelicans are among the largest birds in the world, with the brown pelican's wingspan reaching up to seven and a half feet. A distinctive large pouch hangs from its extremely long bill, and this pouch serves as a net when pelicans crash-dive for fish. Brown pelicans are vigorous flyers and often fly in a V formation, each bird using the opening in the air created by the wings of the bird ahead to decrease the drag on its own wings. Pelicans can also be seen gliding in long lines within six inches of the water's surface, occasionally brushing the water with their out-stretched feathers. Brown pelicans go through a very complex series of annual plumage changes that continue throughout their lives. We have often found their graceful feathers amid the dried seaweed piles lining the high-water mark. Pelicans also provide us with a favorite game: If you are first to spot an approaching line of pelicans, call out the question *Odd or even?* Everyone else guesses one or the other. When the line flies over, count to see who has correctly guessed an odd or even number of birds.

Sea Urchin • Sea urchins have dozens of long, needlelike spines growing from their shells, and some urchins release a toxin when a spine is bumped suddenly. Off this shore they live on submerged rocky reefs, and only the skeleton, or *test,* is ever found along the beach. A small white dot marks the place where each long spine was once attached. This is a purple sea urchin, one of the most common to the area yet unusual to find unbroken along the shore.

Sharks' Teeth • Sharks grow new teeth as necessary, some-times replacing a tooth as often as once a week. Their old teeth can wash up onshore. They are hard to spot at first, but to the practiced eye the small, dark, triangular shape stands out against the curves of shells.

Abandoned Raft • The island country of Cuba lies 90 miles off the coast of Florida, in the Caribbean Sea. In 1959 the Cuban revolution and the rise of Fidel Castro led many people to attempt to escape the now-closed borders of that country. Over the decades many Cubans have attempted to cross the open seas in secretly constructed, primitive boats in hopes of finding asylum in the United States. In 1994 rumors of relaxed immigration policies sent a new wave of refugees to sea in rafts as simple as this burlap-covered tractor inner tube. Many of these refugees were intercepted by the U.S. Coast Guard and returned to Cuba or delivered to Miami. Some did not survive the dangers posed by heat, sharks, and lack of fresh-water. This is only one of dozens of rafts our family has found along this coastline.

Ropes, Etc. • Huge tangles of ropes wash up, lost from fishing boats, cargo ships, or pleasure boats. We have also found small items lost at sea, like silverware and plates, as well as a suitcase, a railing from a yacht, and once, an entire fishing boat caught on a strong tide and beached on the sand. Not all things are lost accidentally. Large tankers sailing in the Gulf Stream often illegally pump their bilges at night, sending tons of black tar into the ocean, and clumps of it wash up onto reefs and beaches. City garbage boats dump trash in the deep ocean, where only some of it sinks. Much of the buoyant plastic eventually floats ashore. Along the way the soft, submerged, clear plastics may be mistaken for jellyfish by marine life in search of food. Once eaten, plastic can suffocate the animals.

Things Too Big to Carry Home

Water • Oceans cover 71 percent of the earth, connecting all species through the great hydrocycle of rising and falling water. Huge amounts of water vapor escape into the air daily, traveling as clouds over land and releasing necessary rain across entire continents. The clouds traveling over this part of Florida are gigantic, and in the summer you can see them delivering a wash of rain out at sea nearly every day. Although the oceans are enormous in scale, our growing human population must give greater care to considering what goes into the water, whether it's invisible chemicals or mounds of very visible garbage. About half the species of plants and animals on our planet (excluding insects) live in the oceans, and the survival of life in the sea *and* on land depends on the constant circulation of clean water.

Sun • As you stand on the east coast of Florida at dawn and look east across the Atlantic Ocean, the earth will rotate toward the sun. On the water's horizon you will see a brightening, then the early arc of a burning ball of fire. The earth's rotation never stops, and steadily the full circle of the sun moves up into the sky. From the beach it looks as if the sun is rising up out of the sea itself. Nearly all the plants and animals in the ocean live within 330 feet of the surface of the sea, where sunlight, necessary for food and energy, is plentiful. The remaining 90 percent of the ocean is too deep for sunlight to penetrate.

Moon • The waters of the oceans are attracted by the moon's invisible gravitational pull as the moon passes overhead. This gravitational pull causes a bulge in the water as it swells and gathers to meet the moon, and the water rises onshore to create a high tide. All around the planet the oceans rise, like a circling wave, to follow the moon's rotation. The earth's rotation causes a corresponding bulge in the earth's waters directly opposite the moon's high-tide pull. This is why you will see two high tides on a particular beach between moon risings. The moon reappears every 24 hours and 50 minutes, and this cycle of high-and-low water marks continuously circles the earth, following the moon's course. The sun's gravitational pull also plays on the tides. Although the sun is larger than the moon, it is farther away, and this lessens its effect. Full moons and sun-moon alignments can cause tides to be higher than normal. Most beachcombers try to go walking soon after a high tide, when the receding water has left new things on the beach to find.

Waves • A wave's pace and size are created by the friction of wind blowing across water. Waves are produced in sets, not individually, and their size is determined both by the strength of the wind and by how much unobstructed water the wind is free to pass over. (The wider the water surface stretches, the larger the waves can grow, which is why lakes and ponds create only small waves.)

The largest waves are found in the open ocean and, on windy days, can often be seen breaking as far out as a mile from this shoreline. Three submerged offshore reefs prevent these huge swells from ever reaching the beach here. When a wave approaches shore, it begins to slow down as the lower part of it drags upon the sea bottom. The upper part continues forward and finally curls over and breaks. The energy the wave has carried from the open ocean is quickly dissipated as the wave sends foam rushing up the sandy beach. If a lot of shells are present you can hear them rolling and clicking together as the wave recedes.

Sand • Our family's house is perched on the edge of the dunes, the sand hills that border the beach itself. This beach is actually part of a barrier island that sits just off the mainland of Florida, one of a string of small islands that runs along the U.S. Atlantic coast. Plants grow along these dunes, adapting to the sandy soil and high salt content of the air and water. These plants help hold the sand dunes in place and mark the line between beach and inland habitats.

The tiny grains of sand along this stretch of shoreline are made of two kinds of particles. Some of the sand grains are bits of quartz. These grains have come from far-inland rocks and have been ground to bits in a long, slow river journey to the ocean. Tides and currents move the sand grains from the mouths of rivers to the Florida shore. But much of the sand on this Atlantic beach comes from fragments of skeletons and shells of sea creatures that have tumbled to shore in the last 13,000 years.

Remembering to Look: Plants and Trees

Periwinkle • This hardy plant grows in full sun, in almost any soil, and has a high tolerance for wind and salt spray. The five-petaled flowers can be white, rose, lavender, or white with a deep red center. They bloom throughout the year and are found in abundance just inland from the beach dunes.

Hibiscus • The hibiscus flower is a common sight in south Florida, growing well behind the dune and bluff areas. The hibiscus originally came from the Pacific Islands, India, and China. Its deep green leaves offset the vibrant colors of the flowers, which bloom only for one day, opening in the morning and closing in the evening.

Beach Sunflower • This low-growing plant spreads over sandy soil and can grow right down to where the dunes meet the beach. The yellow flowers, with deep-maroon-to-brown centers, look like a tiny version of the giant sunflower. Beach sunflowers require very little freshwater to survive.

Beach Morning Glory • These long, trailing vines grow down the dunes to the very edge of the high-water mark, turning and branching as they go. The leaves are a thick, deep green and are broadly notched at the base. Bright purple-pink flowers open in the early morning and close in the afternoon, lasting only one day. They bloom primarily in the summer. This plant is found all over the tropical beaches of the world, and in Thailand it is used to treat jellyfish stings.

Coconut Palm • The graceful coconut palm can reach heights of 65 feet. During a year a tree may produce 50 to 100 large coconuts, which are actually single seeds. These seeds drop off and are quite buoyant, often drifting thousands of miles before lodging in warm sands above the high-water mark. A coconut tree reaches maturity in 10 to 20 years, and can live 80 to 100 years.

If you shake a coconut and hear the sound of liquid washing back and forth, it is likely that coconut milk is still inside. We have often split open a coconut and eaten the white nutmeat that clings to the inner shell. A coconut can be planted in sandy soil with the top of the nut slightly exposed. The coconut palm in the photograph on the back flap of the jacket of this book was grown from a coconut washed ashore, just like the one pictured in the story.

Sea Oats • Sea oats grow along the dune closest to the sea throughout this part of Florida. Long seed heads sway on thin, six-foot stalks that shoot up from tall green grass. By late summer and early fall, these seed heads are heavy with graceful spikelets that move in the wind. Sea oats spread in clumps and grow well where sand is drifting, so they are often planted to help stop erosion. They are remarkably hardy and can even tolerate occasional inundation by the saltwater high tides. Their role in erosion prevention is so important that it is against Florida state law to cut the beautiful seed heads.

Sea Grapes • Sea grapes grow above the ocean's high-water mark and catch sunlight through large, round, sturdy leaves with distinctive red veins. The plants produce clusters of hard grapes that turn purple when mature, and our family has often made jelly from them. Their seeds are salt-tolerant, and they float all over the Tropics, taking root even in drought conditions. The seeds are also scattered by animals that eat the ripe fruit and leave droppings in the sand. Like sea oats, sea grapes can grow on the first dune and are extremely helpful in preventing erosion from wind and water.

Saw Palmetto • On the bluff behind the sand dunes grows Florida's most abundant palm, the saw palmetto. Rarely reaching more than six feet in height, saw palmettos sprawl across the sandy soil in dense clumps, and their sharp, pointed leaves shoot out of the ends of long, spiked stems. Small white flowers bloom on their stalks. The pollen from these flowers is harvested by bees and made into thick palmetto honey.

Illustration Notes

From 1991 to 1996 I took hundreds of photographs along the ocean in Vero Beach, Florida. I took most of these pictures with a simple 35mm Olympus Stylus Infinity camera, much like anyone visiting the beach might take snapshots. (In my enthusiasm for waves and sunrises I dropped two cameras into the ocean while making this book!) The mixed-media collage illustrations in *Out of the Ocean* include photocopies of these photographs, still-life photographs of actual objects, and two kinds of cut paper— Canson paper for the flat color and hand-embellished paste paper for the waves. (To pattern this paper I rolled a brayer filled with tiny dots across wet paste.) The images incorporating shells, sea glass, and other actual objects were made in several steps. Each page of objects was first arranged in a tray of sand and photographed, carefully leaving space for the later addition of other elements. These still-life images were then combined with photographic images of the paper cutouts. Finally, the framed illustrations of the silhouetted figures were added, along with the text.

Jim Henkel was instrumental in solving the technical photographic challenges this method presented. Without his shared love of Florida and his steady encouragement over the years, I might have lost heart. Michael Farmer, designer extraordinaire at Harcourt Brace & Company, helped immeasurably in translating this illustration process to the actual printed page.

DEBRA FRASIER

A few Ocean Journal photographs were contributed by friends and family members, and these people are gratefully acknowledged as follows: Cuban raft, pelicans—Millie Bunnell; sea glass, all portraits of Debra Frasier—Jim Henkel; loggerhead turtle hatchling—Dean Bagley. Back jacket flap: beach house steps (circa 1979)—Kent Larson.

Debra Frasier with a female loggerhead turtle

It is important to note that the photographer waited until the turtle had successfully nested and was returning to the sea before taking this picture.

DEBRA FRASIER grew up in this house at the foot of Beachcomber Lane, where the sandy front steps ran down to the Atlantic Ocean. Loggerhead turtles nest on these beaches, and as a young girl Debra once carried tiny hatchlings to the sea, shooing away attacking seagulls and ghost crabs.

Author and illustrator of *On the Day You Were Born,* the beloved book that welcomes each child to our earth, Debra lives in Vero Beach, Florida, with her husband, photographer James Henkel, and their daughter.